I Can Play a Computer Game

Richard Tan

Rosen
REAL
READERS

Rosen
Classroom™
New York

I like to play games on my computer. Some games help me learn new skills. I learn about math and art. Computer games are a great way to learn and to play.

Some games teach me about the world.

I am learning about animals in **Africa**.

I pretend that I am seeing Africa with

a **hippo**.

Sometimes I use a game **controller** when I play. A controller can make computer games easier to play.

Some games teach me how to draw. In this game I use a tool called a **stylus**. A stylus draws on a screen. It helps me learn illustration skills.

It is fun to play computer games with my brother. He helps me with math games. He teaches me different ways to solve problems.

My grandpa and I play games together.
He did not have computer games when
he was young. I learn a lot when I play
with him.

Some games help me learn about science. This game helps me understand how plants grow.

My sister and I like to play driving games.

Her car is faster. She also drives better.

She usually wins.

Sometimes I pretend that I am a fighter pilot. It feels like I am inside a real fighter plane. I get to fly my plane above the clouds!

Computer games are fun, but it's also good to play outside. If we play computer games for too long, my mom tells us to go play other games outside and get **exercise**.

Glossary

Africa   One of the seven continents of the world.

controller   A device you use to play a computer game.

exercise   An activity that makes you use your muscles to stay healthy.

hippo   A big animal that lives in Africa. Hippo is short for hippopotamus.

stylus   A tool used for writing and illustrating.